HUMBER
SHIPPING

The *Passat*, a steel, four-masted bark built in 1911 by Blöhm und Voss of Hamburg for F. Laeisz & Co. One of the famous 'flying Ps' (*Pamir*, *Pommern*, etc.), she was bought by Gustaf Erikson of Mariehamn, Finland. Seen here under tow on the Humber, *c*.1932.

HUMBER SHIPPING

Arthur G. Credland

TEMPUS

Acknowledgements

This volume and all the royalties are dedicated to the Hull Maritime Society which has supported the Hull Maritime Museum for a quarter of a century. A special thank you to Carole Barley for translating my hieroglyphics!

All pictures, unless otherwise stated, are from the Hull Maritime Museum.

First published 2001
Reprinted 2004

Tempus Publishing Limited
The Mill, Brimscombe Port,
Stroud, Gloucestershire, GL5 2QG
www.tempus-publishing.com

British Library Cataloguing in Publication Data.
A catalogue record for this book is available from the British Library.

ISBN 0 7524 2358 4

Typesetting and origination by Tempus Publishing Limited.
Printed in Great Britain.

Contents

Introduction

This volume mostly illustrates the ships associated with the city of Hull which since the fourteenth century has dominated the Humber region. The town grew up at the confluence of the river Hull, which gave its name to the settlement, and the Humber. In 1299 Edward I, in recognition of the strategic importance of the town for his invasion of Scotland, granted a royal charter. Thus it became the King's town and the full 'Sunday best' name remains Kingston-upon-Hull.

While craft remained small they were able to use the many creeks and havens on both banks of the Humber. Some of these were rivals of Hull, notably Ravenser Odd, destroyed as a result of the periodic erosion of Spurn Point. Hedon also vied with Hull until its modest haven silted up. York, the county town, the seat of an Archbishop and an ecclesiastical and civil administration centre, was a magnet for trade and easily accessible up the Ouse, though a considerable distance from the sea.

Using local timber brought down the Yorkshire river system and imports from the Baltic, the Humber and its immediate tributaries were obvious sites for shipbuilding. Stocks could be set up on any reasonably flat piece of land along the river banks, the raw materials brought by boat and the finished craft launched directly into the water. As well as the whole gamut of trading vessels, wooden vessels were being made for the Royal Navy, from the seventeenth to nineteenth centuries at Thorne, Hessle, Hull and Paull. During the late nineteenth century, Earles shipyard in Hull continued this tradition and built steel warships, including two cruisers; post-war, the Beverley, Selby and Hessle yards all built a variety of specialist craft to Ministry of Defence contracts, from tugs to coastal minesweepers.

In the 1820s the Aire & Calder Navigation Co. established their company town at Goole with dock facilities where cargoes could be assembled for entry into the waterway system, and transferred to and from barges for import, export or transport overland. Goole developed and survives even now as a port in its own right, but Hull was the major focus of the great network of rivers and canals which fed into the Ouse and Humber. Hull docks benefited largely from the products of the industrialisation of the North and Midlands. The imported goods and foodstuffs fed through Hull back into Britain helped fuel that process of industrial expansion.

The Old Harbour, the lower reaches of the river Hull, was where the vessels tied up to load and unload at the staithes along its west bank. The staithes, or quays, were under the direct control of the residents who occupied the houses living both sides of the High Street which ran north-south, parallel to the river. Each merchant lived 'over the shop', his house being a combined dwelling and counting house with facilities for handling and storing goods alongside.

The numbers and sizes of the ships grew ever larger and demanded improved berthing, so in 1778 the town's first enclosed dock was completed, under the auspices of the Hull Dock Co. Its construction created a major breach in the medieval defences of wall and ditch and encouraged the rapid development of the Georgian town. Merchants began to leave the High street, leaving it to their clerks, and occupied elegant new town-houses or houses in the country, away from the sights, sounds and smells of trade.

There had been a thriving trade with Europe since the Middle Ages, but the development of Arctic whaling in the mid-eighteenth century was a bonus. It further stimulated shipbuilding and its ancillary trades and added more gold to the purses of rich merchants and shipowners. The business had its heyday in the 1820s when more than sixty barks and full-rigged ships sailed for Greenland waters each season, killing around 600 whales, whose oil and whalebone were worth (at the time) over a quarter of a million pounds. As whaling declined, so the North Sea fishing began to develop, established by the Brixham and Ramsgate men who had sailed north looking for bigger catches as the stocks in the Channel and southern North Sea declined. The 'industrialised' method of fishing, known as the box or fleeting system, was able to supply the demand for cheap protein made by a rapidly expanding metropolis and the manufacturing towns of the north and Midlands.

The opening of the Hull and Selby railway in 1840 provided a direct line to Leeds and the West Riding and a means of conveying perishable goods, including fish, while still fresh. Grimsby was a rival in the fishing trade but Hull, whether fishing in the North Sea or in the distant water grounds (Faroe, Iceland, Norway etc.), generally caught the greatest bulk of fish. Grimsby was also the home of the cargo-passenger steamers of the Great Central Railway in the North Sea trade. Railway vessels operated out of both Goole and Hull and the railway companies began to dominate the whole pattern of trade to such a degree that in 1893 the Hull Dock Co. was persuaded to sell its entire dock estate to the North Eastern Railway Co. Their rivals, the Hull and Barnsley, tried to prevent an NER monopoly by opening their own (Alexandra) dock in 1885, and the two companies later combined to build the King George dock, opened in 1914. Over on the south bank, the Immingham dock had been opened by King George in 1912.

Hull was at the centre of the Empire's oil-seed crushing industry and there were numerous allied trades such as paint-making and the production of cattle cake. There were massive imports of timber and iron and steel shipbuilding was a major enterprise. The construction of steam-ships in the region had been pioneered by Pearsons of Thorne from c1815, with the construction of small river craft for the coastal and North Sea traders. As the vessels grew in size and the wooden hulls were replaced by iron and steel, production moved down-river to Hull and its environs. Earles shipyard, established in 1845, dominated local shipbuilding for the next nearly ninety years. They engined the *Diana* which became the world's first steam-powered whaler, and in 1882 launched the *Zodiac*, the world's first purpose-built steam trawler. Pioneers in the construction of triple-expansion steam engines, their high quality engines and ships helped give the Wilson Line, Hull's biggest steamship company, a lead over their rivals. Swallowing up Bailey & Leetham in 1903, they became the biggest privately-owned steamship company in the world. Sadly the lack of orders during the great Depression lead to the closure of Earles and its subsequent dismantling in 1931-1932.

The city was heavily bombed during the Second World War, the docks and railways being prime targets. Unfortunately the river Humber, which gives Hull its access to the sea, provided an easy guide for the bomber pilots to follow. Trade continued and the dry docks and repair yards were used for refitting the destroyers which escorted the Russian convoys carrying vital war supplies to our allies.

For the duration of the war the North Sea was effectively a no-go area for trawlers, and Fleetwood on the west coast became the home of the deep sea trawling fleet. In any case, many of the trawlers had been requisitioned for use in coastal patrols, convoy protection, anti-submarine and mine-sweeping duties.

After hostilities ceased, the rebuilding of the fishing fleet was a priority to provide a major food resource for a nation still being rationed for all essentials. The skippers enjoyed great success, big catches fetching good prices, enjoying the fruits of an effective six-year moratorium on fishing in many grounds due to the danger of mines and enemy attack. There was an initial boom in the merchant trade too and vigorous repair and rebuilding of dock facilities damaged by bombing. Dock labour problems and the attempts to introduce new methods of working resulted in a succession of strikes and disputes. The introduction of containerised cargoes in the mid-1960s and the development of roll-on-roll-off ships transformed the nature of dock-work and 1982 saw the privatisation of the whole dock system.

There was also a technological revolution in fishing in the 1960s when the first stern fishing vessels arrived in the Hull fleet. Traditionally, the trawl net had been towed from the side and the catch processed on the open deck, the men working up to eighteen hours at a stretch, exposed to all weathers. Now the trawl was towed directly behind then hauled up a stern ramp. The catch was then processed down below, under cover, and could be deep frozen. Freezing the fish meant that vessels could be bigger, stay at sea for longer and accommodate bigger catches than was the case previously, when fish were merely chilled in layers of ice. The maximum length of voyage for a 'side-winder', storing its catch in crushed ice, was three weeks – after which there would be significant deterioration of quality.

Iceland, which relied on fishing as practically its only source of export revenue, gradually pushed out the fishing limits from its shores. After the last of the Cod Wars in 1975-1976, a 200-mile limit effectively excluded foreign vessels from its waters. Most other nations in the northern hemisphere followed suit with restrictions and quotas; it was a disaster for Hull, which had relied on deep-water fishing off Iceland, Faroe, Norway and Russia. There were suddenly too many vessels and too few places to fish –and many trawlers were scrapped or sold. Though fleets at Hull and other British ports are now much smaller, the catching capacity of the stern trawler is huge and the real challenge for the fishermen is how to tackle the decline in stocks due to over-fishing in practically all the major grounds.

The Common Market has strengthened Hull's traditional links with Europe and the liberation of the Baltic states of Estonia, Latvia and Lithuania following the break-up of the Soviet Union has enabled the rebuilding of links going back to the Middle Ages. The cargo-passenger ferries to Holland and Belgium continue to grow and the new generation due to enter service in 2001-2002 will be so big as to be unable to enter King George dock through the lock pit. Instead, like the *Norbank* ro-ro cargo vessel, they will use a new riverside terminal.

Arthur G. Credland
Hull Maritime Museum

One
Boats and Sailing Ships
– Early Days

A Bronze Age (c.1500 BC) boat on the banks of the Humber at North Ferriby, discovered in 1937 by Ted Wright and his brother. This vessel, along with two others later found nearby, are made of planks butted together and sewn with yew withies. Timbers of medieval boats have been found being used as shoring for the old quays on the River Hull, but the substantial remains of a medieval vessel have yet to be discovered in this region.

William Hammond (1727-1793) elder brother of Hull Trinity House, Chairman of the Hull Dock Co. 1793 and founder of the Trinity House Navigation School, which still exists, in 1787. He negotiated the sale to the Admiralty of the two Whitby vessels, which became the *Resolution* and *Adventure* for Cook's second voyage, 1772-1775.

This silver flagon was made to celebrate the launch of the eighty-gun warship HMS *Humber* in 1693, built by John Frame at Hessle Cliff, a site where the northern end of the Humber Bridge now comes ashore (the Wardens and Brethren of Hull Trinity House).

From the seventeenth to the nineteenth century, vessels were built on the Humber (at Hessle, Hull and Paull) for the Royal Navy. This painting records the launch of the forty-four-gun HMS *Hector* in 1743, built at Hessle by Hugh Blaydes.

The HMS *Rose*, twenty guns, built by Hugh Blaydes in 1757. She fought in the Seven Years War and took part in the capture of Havana and Martinique. She was sunk in 1779 to block access to Savannah and prevent the French bombarding the town. This replica, built in Nova Scotia in 1970, is based at Bridgeport, Connecticut, as a sail training ship. Here she is visiting Albert Dock, Hull, July 1996.

The *Bethia* was built by and for the Blaydes family, in a dry dock adjoining their house, on the River Hull in 1784. Acquired by the Admiralty three years later and renamed *Bounty*, the vessel achieved immortality for her voyage to collect breadfruit plants and the resultant mutiny against Captain Bligh.

Hull was a major trading port from the Middle Ages, but only made its first attempts at Arctic whaling in the sixteenth century, reaching a peak in the 1820s. There are many paintings of whaling vessels but this is the only known photograph of a British sailing whaler. Built at Monkwearmouth, the *Lord Gambier* was in the Newcastle fleet, transferred to Hull in 1845 and was sold to Kirkcaldy in 1853.

The whaleship *Truelove* in 1801, shown armed, during the French Revolutionary Wars. Captured during the American War of Independence she sailed a record seventy seasons to the Arctic fishery from Hull, her last in 1868. In 1873 she took a cargo of cryolite (aluminium ore) to Philadelphia where she had been built 109 years before, in 1764.

The whaleship *Diana* of Hull, built at Bremen in 1840 as a trader, made her first Arctic voyage 1856. The addition of a 40hp engine by Earles of Hull in 1857 made her the world's first steam-powered whaler. Lost in 1869 on her homeward voyage she was the last of the Hull whalers.

Humber Keel *Ada*, Capt. J. Gardner, painted by Reuben Chappell of Goole, the classic Humber sailing barge with a pedigree going back to the Middle Ages. These were the last vessels working under sail in the region, after the 1920s most were motorised.

Keels were the link between the Humber ports and the inland waterways that connected Yorkshire and Lincolnshire with the rest of the country. Competition from the railways resulted in the decline of the canal system and ended the life afloat of a skipper and his family. Here a couple haul their boat themselves to save hiring horses.

The Keel *Rosalie Stamp* of Hull tied up at the Horse Wash, Victoria Pier. In the background is the entrance to the River Hull and the bare land, known as Sammy's Point, was once the site of Samuelsons shipyard. Carters and hauliers would refresh their horses by taking them down the ramp into the water.

A 'Billy Boy' (usually ketch-rigged) tied up in the River Hull c.1900. Of the same ancestry as the keel, this was a sea-going vessel used in the coasting trade as well as sailing to the continent and the Channel Islands.

Two
Crossing The Humber

Ferry boats at Barton, Lincolnshire, on the south bank of the Humber, in 1801. Note the substantial inn and a four-in-hand coach to connect with the ferry.

A jug commemorating John Ellerthorpe, Jr, a ferryman who apparently specialised in carrying livestock across the Humber. Cattle, horses and market produce were sailed across the river in quantity as well as passengers.

There were ferries from Hull, Hessle and Ferriby across the Humber but Hull – New Holland eventually became the only route. This is the paddle steamer *Manchester* built in 1876 at Goole for the Manchester, Sheffield & Lincolnshire Railway Co. Measuring 159ft (48.5m) in length and weighing 221 gross tons, she was rated at 80hp.

The offices built on Nelson Street, Hull in 1880, opposite the Victoria (i.e. Corporation) pier, for the MS&L, whose monogram is visible above the clock. Until the end of the ferry service in 1987, passengers bought their tickets in this building.

The Hull Grand Regatta, 28 September 1847. Note the paddle ferry at the pier crowded with onlookers watching the first Royal Yorkshire Yacht Club's Challenge Cup race. The club's first regatta was a major event on the Humber and the RYYC continues in existence but is nowadays based in Bridlington.

The Corporation Pier (or Victoria Pier, after the Queen's visit in 1854) from Nelson Street with the horse wash in the foreground. The upper deck (1881) provided a delightful vantage point for promenaders and the sloping canopies covered the ramps down to where the ferries tied up.

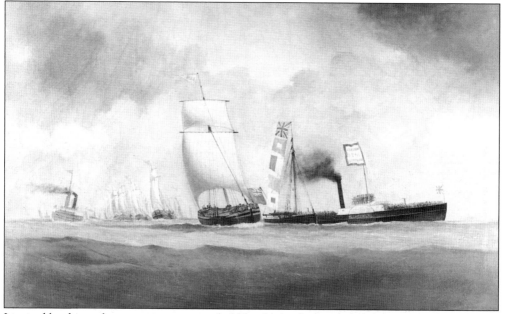

Inspired by the yachtsmen, regattas were held by the keel owners and skippers. In this painting by W.R. Nixon the river steamer *Isle of Axholme* (Gainsborough Union Steam Packet Co.) acts as the mark boat and flies the flag of the Hull Keel Regatta Club 1874. The *Kiero* crosses the finishing line to win the Bailey and Leetham prize.

The paddle steamer *Killingholme*, built by Earles of Hull in 1912, along with her sister ship *Brocklesby*, for the Hull – New Holland ferry service. Each was 195ft (59.4m), 508 gross tons, 98hp and registered in Grimsby for the Great Central Railway Co., successors to the MS&L. During the First World War she was used for coastal patrols, carrying a seaplane which could be craned into the water.

For the opening of the Immingham dock, 22 July 1912, *Killingholme* was painted white and dressed with flags to receive King George V and Queen Mary, who boarded her for a circuit around the dock.

Immingham dock, 22 July 1912. The Lord Lieutenant and official party salute the King and
Queen, who are seated in their car near the royal podium.

Hull – New Holland ferry *Tattershall Castle*, built by W. Gray of Hartlepool in 1934 tied up at Minerva Pier while a car is hoisted aboard. Evidently the pontoon at the adjoining Victoria Pier is out of service. Withdrawn from service in 1972, she became a floating art gallery and is now a pub moored on the Thames.

View across the Humber from the Victoria pier. Hull idlers are watching the ships go by, *c.*1930.

The *Tattershall Castle*, *c.*1950, seen off the eastern wing of the Victoria Pier, in a stiff breeze.

The PS *Wingfield Castle*, sister ship to the *Tattershall Castle*, seen here in the 1990s tied up in Hartlepool where she had been built in 1934. She was 99ft (61m) long, 550 tons, and 151nhp and remained in service until 1974. She has been repainted in her original London and North Eastern Railway colours.

A floating pontoon being towed into position by the tug *Autocrat* in 1937. Tied to the Victoria Pier it rose and fell with the tide allowing easy access to the ferries for passengers and vehicles.

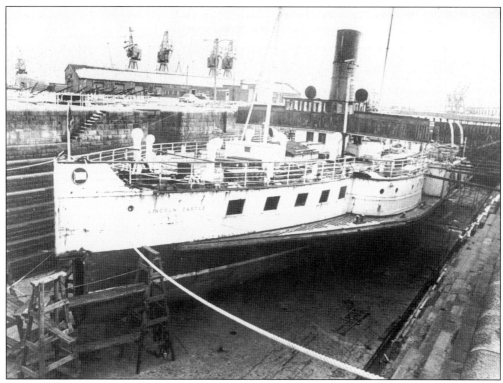

The paddle steamer *Lincoln Castle* in Alexandra dry dock, Hull, 1979. Built in 1940 for the LNER by A. & J. Inglis of Glasgow. Withdrawn from service in 1978, she was the last coal-burning paddle steamer in daily use in Britain. Converted into a restaurant, she was moored near the Humber Bridge in 1979 and later moved to Grimsby where she is still in business.

The *Farringford*, a diesel-electric vessel whose paddle wheels are chain driven. She was built in 1947 for use on the Isle of Wight. Rescued from scrapping, she was transferred to Hull in 1974 after a delay in the opening of the Humber Bridge threatened to leave Hull without a regular cross-river link. She was scrapped when the bridge was completed.

At the New-Holland pier, the *Farringford* on the left, and the *Wingfield Castle* on the right. The ramps for passengers and vehicles are clearly visible and the pier head station which provided a rail link to Grimsby. The pier now functions as a private wharf.

The opening of the Humber Bridge in 1981 (six years behind schedule) resulted in the withdrawal of the ferry service. Seen from the deck of the *Amy Howson*, a Humber sloop which, along with the keel *Comrade*, is maintained and sailed by the Humber Keel and Sloop Preservation Society.

Three

Sailing Ships – A Long Goodbye

The *Return of the William Lee*, a painting by John Ward (1798-1849) of Hull. It shows the vessel entering the Humber dock basin from the Humber. Previously a whaler, she returned from Calcutta in 1839 after reviving the direct trade service between Hull and India.

The bark *Raymond*, a lithograph by John Ward. She was built at Sunderland in 1840 and owned by Thomas Ward. She arrived in Hull in October 1843 with the first consignment of tea direct from China. Previously tea had been transshipped from London.

Humber sloop on the river Hull at Stoneferry *c.*1830. This and the square-rigged keel are the classic local sailing barges. They continued to be built of iron and steel in the twentieth century and were all motorised by *c.*1920.

Throughout the nineteenth and into the twentieth century the coasting smack was the workhorse of the coastal trade along with numerous schooners, brigs and brigantines which also worked across the North Sea. The brigantine *Jean Anderson* was built on Prince Edward Island, Canada, in 1877 and owned by Charles Thompson of Hull in 1909.

The training ship *Southampton* moored off Sammy's Point at the entrance to the River Hull. She was used to train orphan and destitute boys, mainly for service in the merchant navy or Royal Navy. Originally a fifty-gun frigate, built in 1805, she was towed away for breaking at Middlesbrough in 1912. Note the guardship on the left, the old battleship *Audacious*, on station 1890-1894.

Garthpool, the last of the deep sea sailing vessels to sail under the British merchant flag. A four-masted bark of 4,500 gross tons, built in 1881, she sailed from Hull on 23 October 1929, and was wrecked on the Cape Verde Islands, 11 November.

The *Parma* in Victoria Dock, 1933. Another of the four-masted vessels of Capt. Erikson's fleet, used in the Australian grain and wool trades.

The steel four-masted bark *Archibald Russell*, 235 tons, 291ft (89m) long, built by Scott of Greenock in 1905 and sold in 1923 to Capt. Erikson. The last square-rigger to be built in a British yard for a British owner. Upon arrival at Hull, on 27 August 1939, with a cargo of wheat, she was interned for the duration of the Second World War and scrapped in 1949.

Four
Lifesaving, Navigation and Pilotage on the Humber

The first known beacon erected at Spurn was in 1427. Here are the Spurn lighthouses in 1829: the High Light (built by John Smeaton, 1746), a 90ft (27.4m) brick tower and the Low Light, considerably shorter at 50ft (15.2m), together lead vessels safely into the Humber.

Despite the High and Low Lights, the Stony Binks, a shingle bank off Spurn, remained a hazard. Here the troopship *Thomas* is aground on the Binks, 8 June 1821. The oared lifeboat of Greathead type, is pulling alongside and a revenue cutter and three pilot cutters are in attendance.

Spurn is unique in Britain as it has a permanently manned lifeboat station, established in 1810. It is too remote for men to be called sufficiently quickly whether by rocket or telephone. Here the crew wear Capt. Ward's cork life-belt, posing in front of their boat, *c.*1890.

The early lifeboat crews made a living fishing off Spurn; they were a mixture of Yorkshire coble fishermen and Norfolk men using the classic Sheringham crab-boat, characterised by having ports for the oars rather than thole-pins or row-locks.

CARTE'S LIFE BUOYS IN USE.

Adopted by the Comptroller General for Service of Her Majesty's Coast Guard; the Brethren of the Trinity-House in London; several of the principal Steam Packets, and nearly all the Life-Boats in the United Kingdom.

Nᵒ 1
Buoy thrown from Lighthouse & seized by the man.

Nᵒ 3
Having so done supported by the Buoy

Nᵒ 2
Pressing the Buoy downwards to come over the head

Rescue and lifesaving methods were the subject of great experimentation during the nineteenth century. Alexander Carte, ordnance store-keeper at the Hull Citadel for twenty-eight years, devised the familiar cork life-belt with rope hand holds. He died in 1853, aged sixty.

A rocket cart, a familiar sight until the 1920s. It carried the rockets, launching tubes or ramps, tripods and breeches buoy apparatus which could be taken to the most appropriate point on the coast from where the distressed vessel could be reached.

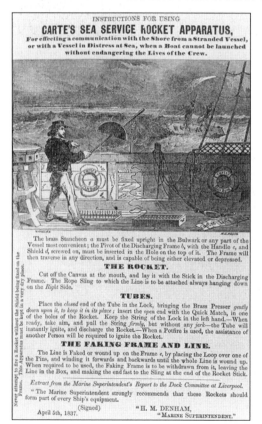

INSTRUCTIONS FOR USING
CARTE'S SEA SERVICE ROCKET APPARATUS,
For effecting a communication with the Shore from a Stranded Vessel, or with a Vessel in Distress at Sea, when a Boat cannot be launched without endangering the Lives of the Crew.

The brass Stancheon *a* must be fixed upright in the Bulwark or any part of the Vessel most convenient; the Pivot of the Discharging Frame *b*, with the Handle *c*, and Shield *d*, screwed on, must be inserted in the Hole on the top of it. The Frame will then traverse in any direction, and is capable of being either elevated or depressed.

THE ROCKET.

Cut off the Canvas at the mouth, and lay it with the Stick in the Discharging Frame. The Rope Sling to which the Line is to be attached always hanging down on the *Right* Side.

TUBES.

Place the *closed* end of the Tube in the Lock, bringing the Brass Presser *gently down upon it*, to keep it in its place; insert the open end with the Quick Match, in one of the holes of the Rocket. Keep the String of the Lock in the left hand.—When ready, take aim, and pull the String *firmly*, but without any *jerk*—the Tube will instantly ignite, and discharge the Rocket.—When a Potfire is used, the assistance of another Person will be required to ignite the Rocket.

THE FAKING FRAME AND LINE.

The Line is Faked or wound up on the Frame *e*, by placing the Loop over one of the Pins, and winding it forwards and backwards until the whole Line is wound up. When required to be used, the Faking Frame is to be withdrawn from it, leaving the Line in the Box, and making the end fast to the Sling at the end of the Rocket Stick.

Extract from the Marine Superintendent's Report to the Dock Committee at Liverpool.
"The Marine Superintendent strongly recommends that these Rockets should form part of every Ship's equipment.

(Signed)   "H. M. DENHAM,
April 5th, 1837.   "MARINE SUPERINTENDENT,"

Never attempt to fire a Rocket without the Shield being fixed on the Frame. This Apparatus must be kept in a very dry place.

Carte also invented a life-saving rocket, used extensively on the east coast, which could be used ship-to-shore or shore-to-ship to carry a line between the two. His prototypes were modified Congreve war rockets. Carte received a bronze medal for his devices at the Great Exhibition, 1851.

The Humber is a difficult river to navigate with shifting mud and sand altering the channels day by day. The licenced Humber Pilots celebrated their bicentenary in 2000 and this company of self-employed pilots still provides the men to guide vessels into and out of the river. This is the Pilot Office near the pier in Nelson Street, Hull, built 1819.

Pilot schooner No.3, the *Dracoena*, was built in 1872 at Cowes as a yacht for West Country owners and came to the Humber in 1890. She continued until the turn of the century and is notable as the river's last pilot vessel under sail.

The steam pilot cutter No.1, *J.H. Fisher*, was built by Earles of Hull in 1931, last but two of the vessels constructed there before the yard closed in the Depression. It was stationed off Spurn to provide a floating base for pilots leaving and boarding vessels at the river mouth.

The beautifully panelled interior of the *J.H. Fisher*. She provided accommodation for thirty pilots and was equipped with two motor-powered boarding vessels. She was 140ft (43m) long and 461 tons.

During the First World War a railway was built at Spurn conveying building materials to construct defences and later to carry munitions and provisions. The workmen, together with the lifeboat crew, found they could propel a rail bogie under sail at considerable speed the length of Spurn Point.

As part of the coastal defences Haile Sands and Bull Forts were built to protect the approaches to the Humber. This is part of the upper deck of Bull Fort, not completed until the very end of the First World War, but recommissioned for the Second World War.

The *Humber Guardian,* built in 1962 by Dunstons of Hessle to use as an inspection vessel for buoys and navigation marks. From *c.*1812 to 1908, Humber navigation was in the control of the Hull Trinity House and, for the next sixty years, the Humber Conservancy Board. Since 1968 the dock authority, now Associated British Ports, has taken this role.

Spurn Lightship, built in 1927 by the Goole Shipbuilding and Repairing Co., here seen in dry dock. She was moored off Spurn using a 26cwt (1.3 tons) mushroom anchor. Transferred to the Bull Station in 1959, she was decommissioned in 1975, and is now a museum vessel displayed in the Hull Marina.

The first floating navigation mark was put at Spurn in 1820. This, the Hebble Light, is probably the oldest surviving lightship lantern in Britain and was carried on the Hebbles Lightship (near Paull) from 1839 to 1846. Light was provided by six large candles. (Hull Maritime Museum).

The Spurn lifeboat *City of Bradford IV*, built by Halmatic of Havant in 1977 at a cost of £200,000; her naming ceremony took place in King George Dock in September of that year. She was an Arun class vessel, 54ft (16.5m) long, with 460hp twin diesel engines.

Five

Shipbuilding on the Humber

The Union Dry Dock, c.1980 was established in 1805 by William Gibson for shipbuilding and repair. On the east side of the River Hull, the lock gates open into the river opposite the old dock offices. The modern building in the background is Hull College.

HMS *Anson*, built at Paull (immediately east of Hull) by Thomas Steemson. She was a seventy-four gun ship launched in 1812, her construction recorded by local artist Robert Willoughby. Steemson moved to Paull from Thorne in 1811.

As early as 1778, Fourness and Ashton built a steam boat which plied briefly between Hull and Beverley. In 1812, the *Caledonia*, built on the Clyde was the first steam packet to operate on the Humber, between Hull and Selby. The PS *Kingston*, above, built by Pearsons of Thorne in 1821 for the Hull Steam Packet Co. was the city's first sea-going steamer, seen here off Yarmouth in the London trade, 1824.

The figurehead of the PS *Sirius* (Hull Maritime Museum). In 1838 she was the first steamer to complete an east-west transatlantic crossing entirely under steam power. She came to Hull in 1840 to have new boilers fitted by Messrs Pim and Gibson's, the dry dock was also lengthened prior to 1842 to accommodate her.

Sirius arrived in New York on 22 April 1838, having left Cork on 4 April. She beat Brunel's *Great Western* by four hours, to his eternal chagrin, since his vessel covered the distance in four days less than the *Sirius*, but had the misfortune of starting out just a little too late!

The figurehead of the paddle-steamer *London* built for the Hull Steam Packet Co. in 1823 but the following year chartered by Gee and Co. for the Hamburg route. After a year she returned to costal trade sailing between Hull and London . Originally 107ft (32.6m) and 107 net tons, she was extended to 120ft (38.5m) in 1842 and scrapped in 1861.

Charles and William Joel Earle began in 1845 as engineers, millwrights, ships and general smiths after taking over Livingstone's foundry. In 1851, they rented land adjoining Victoria Dock and on 15 March 1853 launched their first vessel, the *Minister Thorbecke*, for the Zwolle Steam Navigation Co. This plate is the only surviving image of this vessel.

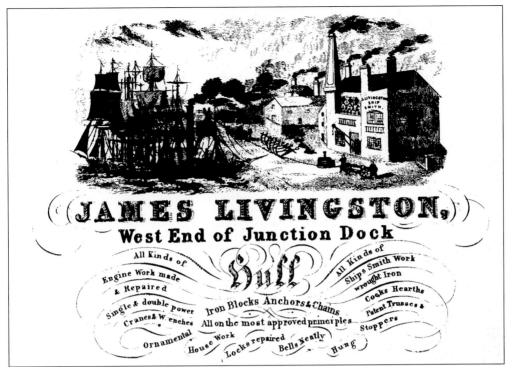

The trade card, *c.*1840, of James Livingstone of Junction foundry situated in Waterhouse Lane, adjoining the Junction (later the Princes) dock. As well as engine-building and all kinds of shipwork, the firm manufactured domestic and ornamental pieces too.

The steam ship *Helena Sloman* built by T. and W. Pim, Alfred Street, Hull, in 1850 for Robert Sloman of Hamburg. Put in the transatlantic trade she was lost on her second voyage to New York. In 1843 Pims had launched Hull's first screw-driven steamer, the *Archimedes*.

The SS *Hawk*, 181ft (55m) and 383tons was launched as yard no.7, by Earles in 1855 for J.B. Ringrose, shipowner of Hull. The Ringrose family were active in the Hull – Netherlands trade in both sail and steam.

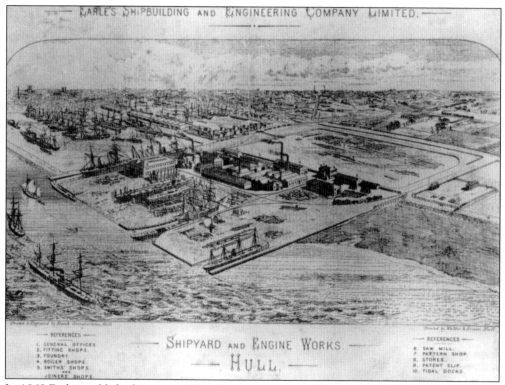

In 1863 Earle established a new yard on forty-seven acres adjoining the Humber bank. Vessels could be launched directly into the river, avoiding the restrictions of the old dock site. After the deaths of the Earle brothers (1870-1871), a new joint stock company, Earles Shipbuilding and Engineering Co., was established with Sir Edward James Reed, who had recently resigned as chief constructor for the navy, as chairman.

1873 saw the building of the 160-ton steam yacht *Slavyanka* for the Tsarevitch of Russia, Grand Duke Alexander Alexandrovitch who was present for the launch. Used by him for a visit to the Prince of Wales at Cowes, he then placed another order for the 800-ton *Czarevna* (above) launched by Cissy Reed, the chairman's daughter, in 1874.

The SS *Bessemer*, also launched at Earles in 1874, was a double-ended vessel with two sets of paddles, 350ft (106m) long, 1,886 gross tons. Designed by Edward Reed for the Bessemer Saloon Steamship Co., she was intended for the Hull – Calais service of the London, Chatham and Dover Railway Co.

Far too large and unwieldy for the channel ports, *Bessemer* seriously damaged the Calais pier and also collided with Dover pier, which was fifty feet shorter than her! She was quickly withdrawn from service and scrapped, and the Bessemer Co. went into liquidation, owing the builders £17,000.

The unique 'swinging saloon', designed by Sir Henry Bessemer, steel magnate and director of Earles, was never put to the test. Luxuriously appointed, the 90ft (27.5m) long saloon was supported on four hydraulic jacks linked to a gyroscope so as to counteract the rolling of the ship. Bessemer was stimulated to this invention because he was a martyr to sea-sickness.

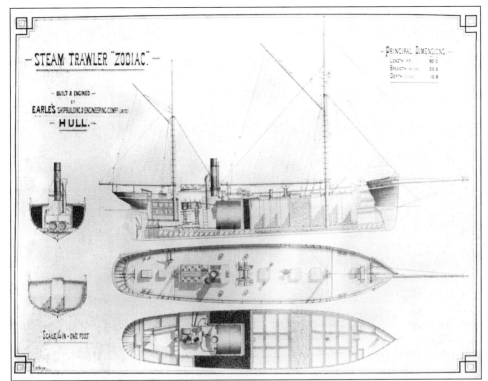

The *Zodiac*, launched in 1882 for the Grimsby and North Sea Steam Fishing Co., was the world's first purpose-built steam trawler. She was 93ft (28.3m) long, 114 gross tons, and carried a full set of sails which helped to economise on fuel and extend her range.

Reed's naval background led to contracts for Earles to build warships for the Turkish, Chilean and Haitian navies. As a result of Lord Hamilton's new defence scheme of 1889 an order was received for two first class cruisers for the Royal Navy; *Endymion* was launched by Lady Salisbury in 1891 and *St George* (above) the following year.

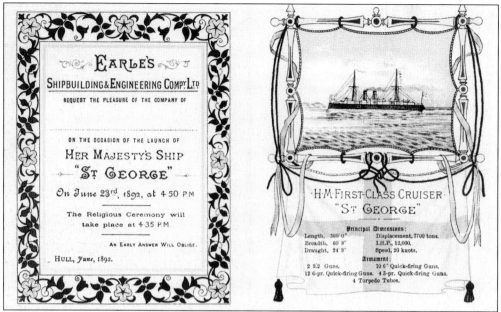

An invitation to the launch of HMS *St George* on 23 June 1892 by Lady Hamilton, in the presence of her husband and other dignitaries. The bottle of wine refused to break until Lady Hamilton picked it up and hurled it against the ship's side. Length 360ft (110m), displacement 7,700 tons with two 9.2in guns, twenty-six quick-firing guns and four torpedo tubes, she was active on the China station's part of Imperial gun-boat diplomacy.

The SS *Dresden* was launched by Earles in 1891 for the Great Eastern Railway Co. One of twelve vessels built for this company, she sailed between Harwich and Antwerp. On 13 October 1913 Dr Rudolph Diesel inventor of the engine which bears his name was lost overboard. Renamed *Louvain* for war service, she was sunk by a U-boat in the Aegean on 20 January 1918.

The motor vessel *Thorold*, soon after launching from Earles yard 1930 for the Quebec and Ontario Transport Co. As a result of the Depression productivity slowed down considerably after 1925. *Thorold* was the only vessel launched that year.

Orders were sought far and wide and a lake steamer *Ollanta* was built for the Peruvian Corporation in 1931. Delivered in a dismantled condition, the components were delivered by rail to Puna near the shores of lake Titicaca and assembled under the direction of W.R. Smale. Observers included the Prince of Wales, the future Edward VII.

The *Ollanta*, afloat ready for trials with the construction gang posing for photographs. Back in 1906, Earles had supplied the smaller vessesl *Inca*, the parts of which were taken up into the High Andes on mules, since the railway was yet to be built. *Ollanta* still survives, abandoned on the lakeside.

Three more vessels were launched in 1931, the last being yard No.682, the Great Western Steamer *Sir Richard Grenville*. The yard was then closed and completely dismantled; the 100-ton crane shown here, a landmark on the river, was sold for use in Kowloon where it survived Japanese attack in the Second World War.

The Spencer and Gardam shipyard, c.1860, on the west bank of the river Hull, adjoining the entrance to the Queens Dock. Note the vessel outside the gates of the dry dock being careened. The building with the small cupola on top is the old dock offices (1820), latterly a public house, but now vacant.

The Scarr family began building small river craft on the Beckside, up the river Hull at Beverley, but in 1890 moved to a much larger site on the Humber bank at Hessle, just west of Hull. On the east side of the Hessle Haven, vessels could be launched directly into the Humber and fitted out in the shallow haven.

Livingstone and Cooper's yard at Hessle, on the west side of the Haven, opposite Scarrs, active c.1915-1925. They constructed a miscellany of traders, trawlers and also a hospital ship. They and the Dunston yard are immediately east of the old Hessle Cliff site.

Vessels under construction, on the riverside at Livingstone and Cooper's yard, Hessle.

In 1932 Scarrs were taken over by Richard Dunston who had been established up river at Thorne for many years. This aerial view, *c.*1958, shows vessels on the slips, leading into the Humber, including a covered construction area and large quantities of plates and components ready for use. The Haven, once a terminal for the Humber ferries, is shared by small craft.

The Hull Central Dry Dock, the SS *Hessle* under repair. Situated at the mouth of the river Hull, on the west bank, the yard remained in use to the 1980s. From 1994-1997 it was the resting place for the Isle of Man ferry *Manxman*, which was used as a pub and restaurant, but is now vacant.

In 1857 Martin Samuelson set up a yard at the mouth of the river Hull, on the east bank, the former site of the Hull Citadel, the Henrician fortification recently demolished. On one memorable day, 29 October 1863, four vessels were launched, the *Countess of Ripon*, her sister ship *Lightning*, the *Earl de Grey and Ripon* and the steam tug, *Solferino*.

The *Thunderbolt*, built by Samuelsons 1863, she served in the Hull – London and Liverpool – India trades, seen here in the colours of Burgess of Swansea. She was lost on 3 November 1893 at Cape Verde. As a result of cash flow problems, the yard closed but reopened in 1864 as the Humber Ironworks, which failed two years later. The site was purchased by Bailey & Leetham to use for ship repairs.

Cook, Welton and Gemmell were established in 1883, occupying part of the Samuelson site. On Wednesday 21 January 1885 their first vessel was launched, the *Precursor*, an iron-hulled fishing smack (sail driven), for Robert Hellyer. Originally from Brixham, Devon, the Hellyers were pioneers of the Hull fishing industry.

During 1885, eight sailing smacks were built but owners were looking to steam power. Also, the steam trawler *Irrawaddy* was built for George Beeching and Thomas Kelsall with engines by C.D. Holmes, a notable Hull engineering company. In 1893 the smack *Bellona* collided with *Irrawaddy* and sank, though all the crew were saved.

In 1902 Cook, Welton & Gemmell moved to the Grovehill shipyard at Beverley, on the river Hull. Yard No.96 was *Viola*, 108ft (33m) long, 174 gross tons, and launched in 1906 for the Hellyer Steam Fishing Co. She was used as a minesweeper during the First World War, then sold to Norway, and in 1926 to a company in Argentina for conversion to a whaling vessel. She was scuttled at Grytviken, South Georgia in 1974; she remains intact but partly submerged.

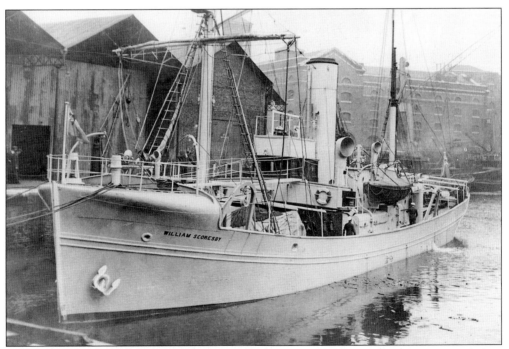

The research vessel *William Scoresby* was launched in 1925 for the Crown Agents. Intended for oceanographic survey in the South Atlantic, she was built around a trawler hull with the interior fitted out for the scientific staff as well as the crew. Escalating costs resulted in bankruptcy but the firm was re-established with C.D. Holmes and Co. (Engineering) as the principal shareholders.

Yorkshire Belle, built at Beverley shipyard in 1947, was a seaside pleasure boat. She sailed out of Bridlington where she is still in service. Seen here on the Hull, off the entrance to the Union Dry Dock.

Yorkshire Dry Dock Co., shipbuilders and ship repairers, part of the Whitaker group since 1917 and situated on the east side of the river Hull, just upriver of North Bridge. The yard has produced tanker barges, oil-rig support vessels, Nile cruisers and here the *Hoocreek* (R. Lapthorn of London) is undergoing repairs. The site was acquired by George Prior (Engineering) in 1997.

Six

Hull Fishing – the North Sea and Beyond

Paull Shrimpers at Hedon Haven on the Humber *c*.1880. These small single-masted fishing craft were named after Paull where many were built or operated from. Each towed one or two beam trawls to catch shrimps or small fish within the Humber estuary. Until *c*.1850 fishing out of Hull and the riverside villages was largely for local consumption.

The prospect of better catches further north brought Brixham and Ramsgate fishermen to Hull in the middle of the nineteenth century. An expanding rail network enabled fish to be distributed around the country while still fresh, supplying a huge demand for cheap protein in an increasingly urban Britain. The ketch-rigged *Regalia* (H 1496) shows the large 80ft (24.3m) vessel which replaced the single-masted smack.

The typical crew of a North Sea fishing smack was five: three men and two apprentice boys, many of whom were orphans. In 1881 Skipper Osman Brand of the *Rising Sun* was arrested for the murder of William Papper, a fourteen-year-old, who was beaten, doused in freezing water and thrown overboard. Brand was hanged at Armley gaol, Leeds, the following year.

Painting of the *Rising Sun* (H 481), 1882. The crews had a hard time working the Box System, smacks stayed at sea for several weeks transferring their catches each morning to a fast steam cutter. They carried on fishing, shooting and hauling the trawl, handling the vessel and boxing and rowing the catch each day – grinding manual work on a diet of fish and potatoes.

After the launch of the *Zodiac* in 1882 Hull trawler owners rapidly converted to steam. Most of the smacks were sold to the smaller British ports or abroad. The box or fleeting system continued even more intensively as it was no longer reliant on the vagaries of the wind. Here boxes are being lowered onto a waiting boat for transfer to the cutter, *c.*1925.

The cutter brought the combined daily catch of the box fleet either to Hull or London for distribution on the railway, supplying the domestic customer and the ever-growing fresh fish and frying trade. Here a vessel of the Hull Red Cross fleet can be seen mingled with assorted tugs outside Billingsgate market, London, c.1925.

The box system had been devised by Hewetts when sailing out of Barking on the Thames and was an efficient way of providing bulk fish to a rapidly expanding market in the country's mushrooming cities. In Hull John Sims (d.1887) promoted the method, which survived until 1936 when Hull abandoned the North Sea to concentrate on deep-sea fishing.

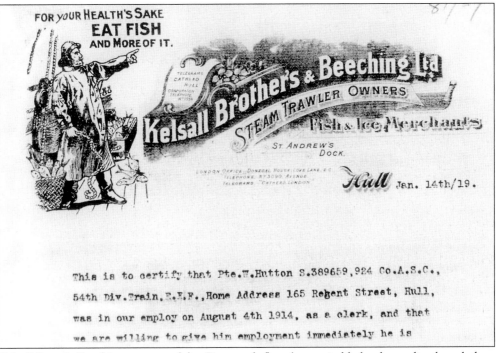

Kelsall Brother's & Beeching Ltd
STEAM TRAWLER OWNERS
Fish & Ice Merchants

St Andrew's Dock.

TELEGRAMS CATHEAD HULL

LONDON OFFICE. DONEGAL HOUSE, LOVE LANE, E.C.
TELEPHONE N° 3090 AVENUE.
TELEGRAMS "CATHERD LONDON

Hull Jan. 14th/19.

This is to certify that Pte.W.Hutton S.389659,924 Co.A.S.C.,

54th Div.Train, E.E.F.,Home Address 165 Regent Street, Hull,

was in our employ on August 4th 1914, as a clerk, and that

we are willing to give him employment immediately he is

Kelsall Bros & Beeching, owners of the Gamecock fleet (recognisable by the cockerel symbol on the funnel) came to dominate the North Sea fleets. In 1921 they merged with their rivals the Hull Steam Fishing and Ice Co., known as the Red Cross fleet because of the St George's Cross insignia.

The *Mino* (H799) of the Gamecock fleet. In October 1903 the Russian Baltic Fleet was passing through the North Sea en route for Asia to meet the Japanese with whom they were at war. On the evening of 21 October, they encountered the Hull Fishing fleet and they started shelling them with quick-firing guns. Fortunately the turret guns could not be brought to bear or the results would have been catastrophic.

The *Mino* in St Andrews fish dock, Hull. The skipper Walter Whelpton, who later died of the effects of shock, rests his elbow on the shell-holed head of the companion way. The trawler *Crane* had been sunk with the death of her skipper and mate.

Thanks to the presence of the Fishermen's Mission (RNMDSF) ship, *Joseph and Sarah Miles*, the injured were treated promptly while still at sea. Ever since the Papper affair, the Mission had increased their support for the fishermen, providing reading matter, extra provisions, tobacco and medical assistance.

The sick bay of the *Joseph and Sarah Miles* was equipped to the highest standard, including a portable Röntgen (X-ray) machine. Dr Anklesaria the medical officer stands at the foot of the examination table.

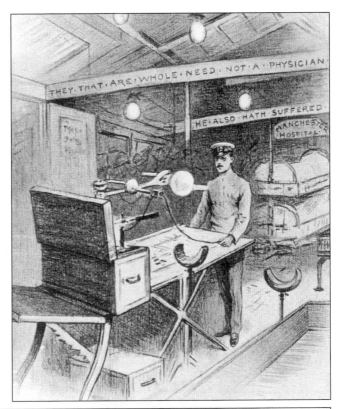

Cortege for the victims of the 'Russian Outrage', passing down the Hessle Road, home of Hull's fishing community. The shop blinds are drawn as a mark of respect. The major international incident was resolved at a tribunal in Paris when the Russian government agreed to pay compensation to the trawler owners, the fishermen and their families.

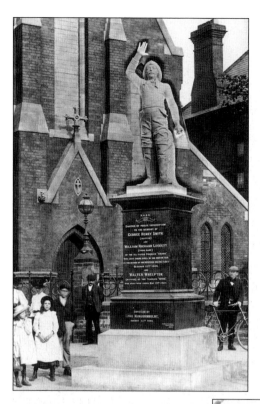

This statue, which still stands, was erected on 30 August 1906, at the corner of Hessle Road and the Boulevard, St Barnabas church in the background. It is a portrait of skipper George Henry Smith, of the *Crane*, and a memorial to him, Walter Richard Leggett the third hand and Walter Whelpton, skipper of the *Mino* who had died 13 May 1905.

The movements of the box fleet and the evolutions involved in the daily off-loading of the catch were under the control of an 'Admiral' or 'Don' Skipper. Instructions were conveyed to the fleet using flags and rockets. Here John Glanville (1881-1941) 'Admiral' of the Hull box fleet holds a sextant; note the gansey, the muffler to prevent his oilskins chafing and trousers of blanket material worn beneath thigh boots.

Hull fish dock, 1930, the roadway behind No.1 Quay. Horses were still employed in large numbers and were a major link in the transport chain but note the Shefflex lorry (RH220). Everywhere there are fish boxes and the open tubs, known as Kits, each holding 10 stone of fish.

In two World Wars much of the fishing fleet was requisitioned for use in coastal patrols, convoy protection and minesweeping. The *Darnet Ness*, built in Beverley in 1920, was used to deal with magnetic mines; she and another vessel towed an armoured cable between them and when current was passed this would create a magnetic field and trigger the mines.

The *Crestflower* and *Lord Brentford*, both built by Cochrane's of Selby in 1930. Seen here completing fitting out in Queens dock, Hull. Shortly before this, the town's first enclosed dock (1778) was filled in. *Lord Brentford* was sold to South Africa and was scrapped in 1966. *Crestflower* was sunk by enemy aircraft in July 1940.

Seven

Hull Traders, Railway Steamers and Some Oddities

The PS *Victoria* (by John Ward), built in 1837 by James North with engines by David Napier for the Hull Steam Packet Co. of Brownlow & Pearson, the company which had originated through the pioneer steamship building of Richard Pearson of Thorne. As a result of 'racing' with its rivals in the prestigious Hull – London run, she suffered two engine-room accidents in 1838 with the loss of fifteen lives.

SS *Tiger* was built in 1857 for Brownlow & Pearson; she was lengthened in 1874 and re-engined. She was acquired by Thomas Wilson, Sons & Co. in 1889 and renamed *Plato* and, in 1896, sold to Furness, Withy of Hartlepool, then to the Antwerp Steamship Co. in 1901 and was finally scrapped the following year.

The SS *Syria* launched in 1881 by Raylton Dixon of Middlesbrough for Bailey & Leetham of Hull, a Hull steamship company established in 1856. She is seen here in Wilson Line colours after the firm was taken over in 1903. Sold to Scandinavian owners, she was sunk by a mine at Borkum on 9 November 1940.

The SS *Jervaulx Abbey* launched in 1908 for the Hull & Netherlands Steamship Co. (formerly C.L. Ringrose & W.H.H. Hutchinson) the year they were taken over by the North Eastern Railway Co. She was an armed boarding steamer during the First World War, then returned to NER in 1920 (from 1923 the LNER), and in 1935 transferred to Associated Humber Lines. She was sunk by the Japanese early in the Second World War.

The SS *Ouse*, built in 1911 for the Lancashire & Yorkshire Railway, was used by the Admiralty as a Q-ship in the First World War. In 1922, ownership was transferred to the London & North Western Railway Co. the LMS in 1933 and AHL in 1935. She was sunk following a collision in 1940.

The SS *Accrington* was launched in 1910 for the Great Central Railway Co. (formed in 1897 from the old Manchester Sheffield & Lincolnshire Railway Co.) with the intention of 'competing' in the North Sea trade, sailing Grimsby – Hamburg and Grimsby – Antwerp. GCR became part of the LNER in 1923 and from 1935 the steamer was operated by AHL.

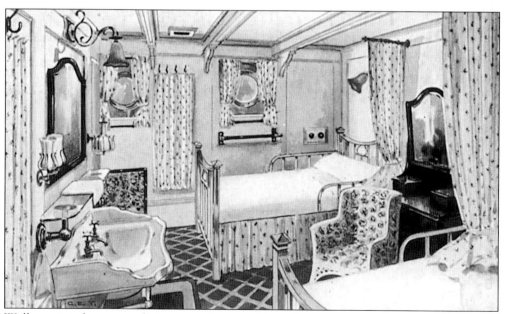

Well-appointed accommodation was a feature of the railway steamer as shown in the publicity postcards. In 1942 the *Accrington* was used as a rescue ship for the North Atlantic convoys; she escorted forty convoys and saved 138 crew. From 1946 she was in the Hull – Antwerp run and scrapped in 1951.

The SS *Duke of Connaught* built in 1902, by John Brown of Clydebank, for the Fleetwood – Belfast run of the Lancashire & Yorkshire Railway Co. Transferred to the LMS in 1928, she sailed Heysham – Isle of Man, and from 1930 sailed Hull (Riverside Quay) to Zeebrugge. She was scrapped in 1934.

The SS *Graphic* was built 1902 by Raylton Dixon of Middlesbrough and acquired by W.H. Cockerline of Hull, who set up his company in 1879. Cockerline was succeeded, after his death in 1941, by his son who wound up the business in 1957. The vessel was a tramp steamer seen here with a large deck cargo of timber.

Maj. Sidney Cotton's (pioneer of aerial reconnaissance) Bellanca aircraft being loaded aboard the *Dettifoss* at Albert dock, Hull, on 5 May, 1931. This monoplane, fitted with skis, was used in the search for the missing Arctic explorer Augustine Courtauld.

The SS *Oberon*, Finland line, on her maiden voyage, 18 August 1925, from St Nazaire (where she was built) to Hull. The marine artist and poster designer Harry Hudson Rodmell was aboard with representatives of J. Good & Son, the Hull agents, and other invited guests. She had accommodation for 132 first and 236 third-class passengers.

The 'Winestead Sludger', devised by Robert Drewery to keep open the Winestead drain, which drains the water off 20,000 acres of agricultural land in East Yorkshire. Weighed down with water ballast at low water it settles on the bottom. When the sluice was opened, the pent up water pushed the sludger toward the river, scraping mud from the bottom and sides of the drain in the process.

The 'roller ship' invented by Ernest Bazin and launched into the Seine at St Denis in 1896. She floated on three pairs of large hollow rollers, each pair driven by an engine geared to a normal propellor shaft and screw. She was steered by a column of water ejected from the stern by a large pump. Designed to give passengers a smooth passage, the project was a costly failure and is seen here after purchase by W.A. Massey of Hull in 1898 for scrapping.

The *David Dale* on the Humber. A twin-screw steam, bow-well, bucket dredger built by Lobnitz at Renfrew in 1905. The bucket ladder was 100ft (30.5m) long and she was 1,562 gross tons.

A pontoon grab dredger at work in Grimsby docks. Note the landmark hydraulic tower in the background, a two-thirds replica of the civic tower in Siena. Water pumped from it operated the lock gates and other dock machinery.

The SS *Sturton* in the Avon gorge, Bristol. Built in 1899 she belonged to the Deddington Steamship Co., founded 1889 by Henry Samman, who operated vessels in the coasting and Baltic trades, from Hull.

The SS *Chelsea* was built in 1925 by the Northumberland Shipbuilding Co. of Newcastle; she is seen here in the Elbe at Hamburg. The owners William Brown, Atkinson of Hull were founded in 1846, and during the 1850s ran a fleet of Arctic whalers. Active latterly in the coasting and Baltic trades they continued as ship-broking and freight-forwarding agents, bought by the Escombe Group (P&O) in 1978.

The SS *Lesrix*, built in 1924, weighing 703 gross tons, seen here under the Clifton suspension bridge, Bristol. The owners, Robert Rix, were founded in the 1880s by a former master mariner to participate in the coasting and Baltic trades. R. Rix ceased operations in 1947 but his son's company, J.R. Rix, still operates a fleet of coasting tankers.

The motor vessel *Mary Birch* (157 tons), a grand old lady built in 1915, she was operated from Hull by the B.W. Steamship, Tug & Lighter Co. in the coasting trade. Sunk in collision with the trawler *Loch Moidart* in the Humber, 1954, she was raised again and passed to the ownership of R. Lapthorn.

Eight
Hull Docks – Old and New

An aerial view of the Town Docks system, c.1950, opening into the river at the Humber dock basin, left. Clockwise, the Humber dock, Princes dock, and Queens Gardens, formerly the Queens dock. The entrance to the river Hull seen on the right; within the circuit is the city's medieval core, including the magnificent Holy Trinity church. Note the New Holland ferry at the pier.

Looking from the lock pit into the Humber dock *c.*1885, the Swedish bark *Atlantic* tied to a dolphin. Behind, with a clock at roof level is the No.7 Warehouse designed by J.B. Hartley for the Hull Dock Co.

The Princes dock opened in 1829 and is seen here in 1920. St John's church, left, was demolished in 1926. The Dock offices, with the three domes, was built in 1871 for the Hull Dock Co. and since 1975 has been the home of the Hull Maritime Museum. The Wilberforce column was moved in 1935 to relieve road congestion.

Sidney Screeton Drewery, one of the divers for the Hull Dock Co.

More famously, William M. Mitchell was a diver at Hull and Tilbury docks, c.1880-1910. Formerly a gunner in HMS *Warrior* and present at the opening of the Suez Canal (1869) in HMS *Bellerophon*. He introduced his wife and daughters to diving, probably the first women to don hard hat and diving suit.

The Queens dock, the city's first enclosed dock, opened in 1778. Note the whaling vessels on the left, one with whale jaw bones hung from the mast, and the characteristically heavy framework for suspending the whaleboats.

The *Success*, built in 1840, served as an emigrant ship until 1872 when she was bought by the Australian government to use as a convict hulk. At the turn of the century this replica visited Europe and America, including a spell in the Queens dock, Hull, in 1900, captured here.

Queens dock was in use for 150 years before becoming too cramped for modern ships. In 1930 it was filled with commercial waste; here a steam lorry dumps slag from the National Radiator Co. Note the trawler *Golden Deep* in the background and the old cannon bollard in the foreground.

A moody picture by Harry Cartlidge, entitled *The last drop of water*, with the silhouette of the Dock offices and Wilberforce monument in the background. Queens Gardens was laid when the dock was completely filled.

Albert dock was constructed to the west of the Town Docks and accommodated both merchant vessels and the fishing fleet. Opened in 1869, this is the lock entrance at the east end (it opens into the Humber) in 1867. Note the traction engine and the massive labour force conveying wheelbarrows over a spider's web of planks.

Victoria dock was constructed to the east of the river Hull in 1850 with an entrance into that river (far left) and a half tide basin and outer basin opening into the Humber. The site on the river bank is that occupied until 1931-1932 by Earles shipyard. The whole of the dock is now filled and covered by a housing development.

Immediately to the east of the Victoria dock is the Alexandra dock, completed by the Hull and Barnsley Railway Co. in 1885 to compete with the North Eastern Railway who dominated the rest of the dock system. Seen here in 1964, it was closed in 1982 but reopened in 1991 following an expansion in trade.

This 100-ton fixed jib crane at Alexandra dock was built by James Taylor of Birkenhead in 1888. Seen here in 1952 lifting a 98-ton casting for a Swedish silicon sheet mill, made by David United of Sheffield. Used intermittently in the 1960s the crane remains as a monument to Victorian engineering.

An aerial view of the Albert Dock, 1958, with the lock pit in the foreground, showing the construction of the new Riverside Quay and associated sheds, the original having been severely damaged by bombing in 1941.

Sadly the landmark Edwardian clock tower was demolished to make way for the new development. Here, c.1945, a portion of the Mulberry Harbour (built for the Normandy landings) is in use as a temporary riverside berth. A train awaits one of the many troop arrivals from Cuxhaven, Germany.

The old Riverside Quay c.1930. It was accessible at most stages of the tide and was used by vessels carrying perishables and the regular North Sea cargo-passenger vessels of the Railway companies. This is the *Duke of Connaught*, built in 1902 for services in the Irish Sea. Transferred to Hull 1930, she was scrapped 1934.

St Andrew's dock, the Hull Fish Dock, c.1946, crowded with trawlers. In the foreground are the *Mendip,* belonging to Charleson-Smith and built 1934, and the *Arab,* built in 1937. The elevated conveyors carry ice directly from the ice factory to the vessel, for preserving the catch at sea.

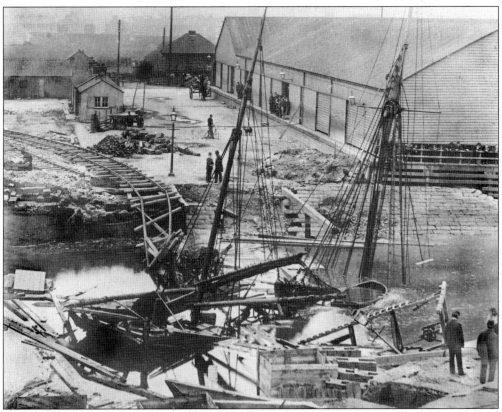

Accommodation was needed for both the North Sea box fleet and the 'Single Boaters' sailing to the deep water fisheries off Iceland, Faroe and Norway. An extension to the fish dock was completed in 1897; during construction the temporary dam burst open, on 15 May 1896, and in the sudden outrush of water into the new dock the smack *Young Greg* was smashed and sunk.

King George dock in 1962. It opened on 26 June 1914 by George V shortly before the outbreak of the Great War; it was the country's first dock to be completely electrified. The water area of fifty-seven acres was extended in 1969 by the opening of the Queen Elizabeth dock. Used by vessels in trade world-wide and the Hull – Rotterdam, Hull – Zeebrugge ro-ro services.

Until the 1960s the Princes dock remained in use for fitting out trawlers built at the Beverley shipyard. Here the *Northella* nears completion in August 1951 alongside the C. D. Holmes (Engineering) workshops.

Nine
Deep Sea Fishing – 1928-2000

Hull was always a pioneering fishing port and the Yorkshire shipyards built high quality trawlers which were in demand overseas as well as in Britain. Here is the *Ceylon Bul Bul* built by Cochranes of Selby. She is outward bound for Ceylon (Sri Lanka) on 31 March 1928.

Steam trawler *Andrew Marvell* (H399) on the slip of the Hull fish dock extension, *c*.1930. Note the large labour force employed on the refit, working from wooden trestles.

The lately-completed reconstruction of the No.2 Fish Market, St Andrews Dock, Hull, was engulfed by fire on the evening of 25 August 1929. Flames spread to the nearby rolling stock and several trawlers in the dock, a dramatic event captured by Harry Cartlidge.

The 'cod farm' in 1933 – an area of land adjoining the Hull fish dock extension where salted split cod was laid to dry in the sun. This supplied an important export trade to South America and the Mediterranean before the Second World War.

The *Arctic Queen* in Hull dock, 29 May 1928. Formerly the *Vasari* she was built at Middlesbrough in 1909, but acquired by Hellyers, trawler owners, for halibut fishing off Greenland. The fish were caught using long lines from dories, the small rowing boats much in evidence here.

The *Hugh Walpole* (H409) leaving the lock pit of the Andrews dock, *c*.1937. Built in that year by Cochranes of Selby she returned to fishing after war service, was renamed *Rossella* in 1951 and scrapped in 1959.

Trawlers *c*.1937, outside the lock pit of St Andrews dock, alongside the offices of the Hull Steam Trawlers Mutual Insurance and Protecting Society, looking out into the Humber. On the right is *Lorenzo*, built in 1933 at Beverley for the Hull Northern Fishing Co. Ltd.

Trawlers in the William Wright dry dock (adjoining Albert dock), Hull. *Orsino* was built at Beverley in 1929 by Cook, Welton & Gemmell for the Hull Northern Fishing Co. Sold to the Dutch in 1936, she was used by the German navy but sunk by British MTBs in 1943. *Tourmaline* was employed as a minesweeper and in 1948 sold to Polish owners.

The *Lady Jeanette* (H466) built in 1937 for the Jutland Amalgamated Fishing Co. While off the entrance to the Hull fish dock, the vessel was caught by the current and sank with little warning on 8 March 1939. Nine men died a few hundred yards from the shore; the German salvage crew brought in to raise her departed unannounced as a result of the impending hostilities.

At the outbreak of the war in 1939 trawlers were requisitioned for a wide variety of military duties. Here a barrage balloon is being hoisted from the *Chrysea* in the Humber, June 1940. Built 1912 by Smiths dock, Middlesbrough, she returned to fishing (from Grimsby) after the war and was scrapped in 1947.

A trawler converted for minesweeping, military number 642, being towed on the Humber by *Tollman*, a vessel belonging to the United Towing Co. of Hull. Note the A-frame mounted on the bows, she was furnished with an acoustic hammer for detonating acoustic mines.

The *Quest* on the Humber, 1944. Not a trawler but the Norwegian whale catcher *Foca 1*, used by Ernest Shackleton for his 1920-1921 expedition to Antarctica. During the Second World War she was used as a water ship for the corvettes based at Immingham.

A fleet of Danish Seine-netters, known as 'snibbies' are gathered in Victoria Dock in May 1945, all flying their name pennants, celebrating the end of war in Europe and the liberation of Denmark.

Arctic Corsair, Boyd Line, Hull; built 1960 at Beverley shipyard, she was finally retired in 1987. She is now moored in the river Hull behind the Streetlife Museum and is open to the public, preserved in original, sea-going condition.

A general view of Hull fish dock in 1950. The fleet grew quickly after the war and catches were excellent since stocks of fish had six years to recover when large areas of the sea were out of bounds for fishing because of the danger of mines or attack from sea and air.

The oil-fired steam trawler *Kingston Jacinth* built in 1951 for the Kingston Steam Trawling Co., she remained in service until 1975. Note the city of Hull coat of arms, three golden crowns, on a blue background, emblazoned on the bow. The fish quay is lined with aluminium kits (tubs) filled with fresh fish ready for auction.

The motor trawler *Princess Elizabeth* (H2380) built in 1952 by Cochranes of Selby for the Boston Deep Sea Fisheries. She was sold in 1959 to Australian owners, at Port Adelaide, renamed *Southern Endeavour* and sank in 1979 when owned by Gulf Seafood of Melbourne.

The diesel electric trawler *Cape Kennedy* being launched at Cochranes of Selby in 1966. Because of the narrowness of the Ouse, like the river Hull at Beverley, vessels had to be launched sideways into the water. Renamed *Ross Kennedy* in 1966, then *Ross Intrepid*, she was sold to the Royal Navy in 1977.

Before departing for the fishing grounds, fresh ice was shot into the fish hold through a pipe leading from a conveyor which brought ice direct from the factory. On the open deck fish was gutted, washed and then packed in the hold, a layer of ice and a layer of fish alternately.

On return to port, the fish was hoisted out of the hold in baskets and swung ashore to be emptied into the kits (tubs), originally of wood, latterly aluminium, each holding 10 stone of fish. Here the 'bobbers' are tidying up after unloading. Stale ice is emptied overboard, on the right are stacks of freshly scrubbed pound boards.

The motor trawler *Lord Nelson*, built by Rickmers Werft of Bremerhaven for Associated Fisheries, arrived in Hull on 30 June 1961, as the port's first stern-fishing trawler. The technique had been pioneered by Salvesens of Leith, inspired by their experience with whale factory ships. The net was towed behind then hauled up a stern ramp. Part of the catch was fresh (i.e. chilled), the rest solid frozen.

The motor trawler. *Junella* leaving St Andrews dock. She had been built for J. Marr and Son, by Hall Russell of Aberdeen in 1962, the first British trawler to freeze the entire catch. After hauling up the ramp the fish was handled under cover – unlike the old side-fishing vessel where the men worked exposed on the open deck.

The *Ross Implacable* (H6) was built at Selby in 1968 for British United Trawlers. She is seen here in the William Wright dock. The stern ramp is clearly visible and the pair of 'trawl doors' which keep the mouth of the net open as it is towed behind. Sold to Iranian owners in 1982, she was renamed *Hamar*. (Author's photo).

Stern trawler *Hammond Innes* (H80) was built at Beverley shipyard in 1972 for Newington trawlers. On her maiden voyage, a twenty-four day trip to the Norwegian coast in January 1973, she landed 1892 kits of fish grossing £25,739. She was sold in 1977 to Canadian interests for conversion to a fishing research vessel.

The stern trawler *Northella* built at Wallsend on Tyne for J. Marr and Sons in 1973. In 1978 she landed 4,579 tonnes of fish and was used by the Royal Navy during the Falklands campaign in 1982 for minesweeping. With declining fishing opportunities she was chartered to Trinity House to use as a guard ship in the Channel while a power cable was being laid. Sold to the Royal Navy in 1983.

Launched as the *Ranger Castor* by Brook Marine of Lowestoft in 1972, she was sunk during a fierce storm off North Cape, Norway. Speculation persists as to the precise cause of her loss. (Photo by Malcolm Fussey)

Portia (H241), the first diesel electric trawler in the Hull fleet, built in 1956 at Middlesbrough for Hellyers. Seen here in 1976 during the Cod War with Iceland, hauling her net with a Royal Navy frigate close by.

After the last Cod War the Icelandic fishing grounds were lost to British trawlers and Russia and Norway also set limits and quotas. The result was a terrible crash with too many trawlers and greatly reduced access to well-stocked grounds. Vessels were sold abroad or scrapped like these two being dismantled at Drapers yard on the Humber.

The Hull fishing effort has recovered since 1976, there are about a dozen large stern trawlers with huge catching capacity but they and the entire fishing effort in the Northern Hemisphere are threatened by declining stocks due to over-fishing. The *Arctic Warrior* seen here in Albert dock (since 1976 Hull's fish dock) is the latest addition to the Boyd Line fleet.

Ten
Tugs on the Humber

Anonymous painting of two wooden-hulled paddle tugs, *Hecla* and *Lightning,*, built in 1865 for Thomas and John Gray of Hull. Shown off Victoria Pier, the manner of execution suggests they were painted from builders drawings.

Steel tug *Englishman* built for T. Gray in 1913 by Henry Scarr of Hessle achieving 9¾ knots and 230ihp. Cut-throat competition threatened to put many Humber tug owners out of business so, in 1920, T. Gray, Premier Tugs, T.C.Spink, Troy Steam Towing, S. Harrison & Humber Steam Towing Co. merged to become the United Towing Co.

Larkspur, built in 1919 as the *West Bay* for the Admiralty and used at the Royal Navy Armaments Depot, Priddys Hard. Sold in 1953 to Peter Forster & Co., she remained in service till 1962.

283 - Bridlington - Steamer Entering The Harbour

Paddle tug *Frenchman* was owned by United Towing 1921-1929. During the summer months she was used as a pleasure steamer out of Bridlington harbour. Built in 1892 by Rennoldsons of South Shields as the *Coquet* and sold to T. Gray in 1899. She was latterly a dumb barge and was broken up in 1968.

The *Empire Stella* was built for the Ministry of War Transport by Cochranes of Selby in 1945 and acquired by United Towing in 1946, renamed *Serviceman*. She was sold in 1969 to Scandinavian owners.

T.I.D. tug, no.98, built by Dunstons at their Thorne yard and engined at Hessle, seen here on trials in the Humber. These all-welded, prefabricated 'utility' tugs were built to a standard pattern by a number of yards and could be completed at the rate of one every $4\frac{1}{2}$ days! Completed in September 1944, she was taken to Burma in 1947.

The *Yorkshireman* was built at Earles shipyard at Hull in 1928 for the United Towing Co., length 120ft, (36.5m) 251 gross tons. After war service she returned to normal duties and in the summer season was used as a pleasure steamer at Bridlington, replacing the *Frenchman*. She was sold in 1965 for scrap.

The *Lloydsman* was built in 1971 by Henry Robb of Leith as an ocean-going salvage tug, achieving 18 knots and 10,000bhp from two internal combustion engines by Crossleys. During the Cod Wars with Iceland in 1973 and 1975-1976 she was employed as a fisheries protection vessel. She was sold to Singapore owners in October 1979.

The twin-unit tractor tug *Faithful* (pennant no. A228) was built by Dunstons of Hessle for the Royal Navy in 1985, length 128ft (39m) and 375 gross tons, achieving 12 knots and 29.63 tons bollard pull. She was one of a series of Adept class vessels for harbour work with sea-towing, fire-fighting and salvage capabilities.

Eleven
Merchant Shipping and the Humber

Built for Salvesens of Leith by Smiths Dock, Middlesbrough, the whale factory ship *Southern Venturer* was launched in 1945 to restart Britains whaling trade with a thoroughly modern vessel. The local connection is the equipment installed for 'cooking' and processing the whale meat and bone, made by Rose, Downs & Thompson, a Hull company noted for its oil-seed crushing machinery.

The *Jaroslaw Dabrowski* of Polish Ocean Lines, Gdynia, built at Blyth in 1950, 557ft (109m) long, 3,196 gross tons and fitted with George Clark triple expansion steam engines. She was the last coal fired cargo steamer to come to Hull and was sold in 1975.

During the Festival of Britain not only was there the major display on the South Bank, London, but a floating exhibition carried around the coast in the aircraft carrier *Campania*. She is seen here entering King George dock 18 June 1951, with the tug *Norman* at the bow. She was scrapped in 1955.

By the end of the nineteenth century, Hull was the world centre of oil-seed crushing. After the Second World War, processing was increasingly transferred to the countries where the oil seeds were produced. However, Palm line vessels were a familiar sight in Hull docks down to the 1980s. The motor vessel *Andoni Palm*, built in 1958, 5,802 gross tons, was a regular in the West African trade.

Even in peacetime it is not all plain sailing! The SS *Lona* caught fire at No.12 Quay, King George dock, with a cargo of pit props in September 1956. Built in 1943, she was registered in Sweden, length 327ft (99.6m), 2,891 gross tons.

Timber was a significant part of Hull's trade for generations, especially from Scandinavia and the Baltic; imports have recently been stimulated by Estonia, Latvia and Lithuania regaining their independence. Here pine boards are unloaded from SS *Lassell* from Buenos Aires at No.21 Quay, Alexandra dock, on 14 January 1958.

The Danish trade in butter and bacon was dominated by the Wilson line and here we have the *Borodino*, unloading at the Riverside Quay, Hull, on 9 November 1959. Instead of the dark green hull of the rest of the fleet, 'butter boats' were painted grey.

The motor vessel *Baltic Star* of United Baltic Corporation, built in 1961 at Rendsburg, 305ft, (93m) long, 1,571 tons, was a regular in the Hull Finnish service, discharging at No.23 Shed, Alexandra dock on 12 February 1962.

Hull has also been a major grain importer. Here in July 1968 grain is being discharged 'overside' to lighters, using suction elevators on floating pontoons.

The Ellerman Bucknall vessel *City of Hull* was built in 1971 by Robb-Caledon of Dundee, 502ft (183m) long, 7,093 gross tons. Here making her first visit to the city whose name she bore on 6 April 1974.

For generations dock work was labour intensive, requiring a large labour force and their manual skills. The men were casual workers and presented themselves at the 'pen' each day for selection by the foreman. Here sacks are being transferred from dockside sheds direct to rail wagons.

Stevedoring requires great skill to organise effective packing and unpacking of a huge variety of cargoes in a ships hold, or setting up the staging for discharge over the side, as in this banana boat *c*.1935. Nowadays most cargoes are containerized and can be lifted mechanically or driven straight on or off a ro-ro ship.

Oil jetties on the Humber, at Saltend, 25 August 1950. On the right *Mette Maersk* is discharging gasoline and kerosene from Curacao and on the left the *Denbydale H* is discharging 10,000 tons of fuel oil from Rotterdam. The little *Shelbrit 10* loads vaporizing oil piped from a shore tank across the *Denbydale H*.

A 72-ton dredger is being loaded from a special road vehicle by the 80-ton floating crane in Alexandra dock on 11 January 1958.

Shore-based pneumatic grain elevators take grain from lighters at King George dock on 24 May 1961.

The new floating suction elevator *Carnaby* discharges grain, 300 tons per hour, from the motor vessel *Otterburn* into lighters at King George dock on 17 August 1962.

The motor vessel *Richmond Castle* in No.1 graving dock, King George dock, on 23 January 1962. Belonging to Union Castle lines, she was built by Harland & Wolff, Belfast, in 1944, 474ft (144.4m) long and 7,960 gross tons.

Discharging 95 tons of Russian furs from SS *Pulkavo* to railway vans at King George dock on 1 September 1966. The cargo, valued at £670,000, was despatched in sealed vans to the London fur sales.

The motor vessel *Spero*, Ellerman's Wilson line, pioneer ro-ro ferry in the Hull – Gothenburg run, 1966, later transferring to Zeebrugge, offered luxury one-class travel for 408 passengers and access by stern ramp for cars, containers and trailers. Sold in 1973 to Greek owners, she operates in the Aegean as the *Sappho*.

The cargo of 16,000 tons of grain from New Orleans is being discharged overside using suction elevators, at King George dock on 5 October 1962, from the *Scottish Trader*, Trader Navigation Co. On the previous day she set a record of discharging 5,975 tons in eleven hours.

A curious cargo – Giraffes brought from Rotterdam for Chester Zoo, in August 1970, aboard North Sea Ferries *Norwave*, a cargo passenger ro-ro ferry.

A roll-on roll-off ferry, the twin screw motor vessel *Baltic Enterprise*, built in 1973, 4,668 gross tons, for the United Baltic Co., London. She is discharging cargo at the Finnish berth, Queen Elizabeth dock, in December 1973.

Docklift 2 barge seen here at Hull in 1974, owned by Big Lift B.V. Dordrecht.

Docklift 2 settles in the dock, lowers the stern ramp and the barges are floated onto it. The system allows transmission of cargoes with minimum involvement of dockers.

Since the Second World War it has been the custom for the City of Hull to adopt a Royal Navy vessel and give the Freedom of the City to the officers and men. The Leander class frigate *Galatea* (built 1963) paid her first visit in 1964 and her last in 1982 when she was decommissioned. Her namesake the cruiser *Galatea* had been a guardship on the Humber 1894-1903.

The *Sir Winston Churchill* (300 tons) a topsail schooner built for the Sail Training Association by Dunstons of Hessle in 1966. She had accommodation for thirty-six trainees and was 135ft in length. She paid her last visit to Hull in October 2000, before being decommissioned.

The *Sir Winston Churchill* was accompanied in Albert dock by the latest STA vessel, the brig *Stavros S. Niarchos*, on her coastwide maiden voyage. Built at Appledore, Devon, she is 187ft (59.4m) long and 483 gross tons, with auxiliary engines and bow thruster for berthing.

The North Sea Ferries service, Hull – Rotterdam was instigated by the cargo-passenger vessels *Norwave* and *Norwind*, in 1965 and 1966. In 1975 the new generation of ro-ro vessels *Norland* (above) and *Norstar* entered service. In 1982 the *Norland* was requisitioned for service in the Falklands as a troop carrier.

The *Norsea* and *Norsun* took over the Rotterdam service in 1987 and *Norland* and *Norstar* transferred to Zeebrugge. *Norsea*, above was built on the Clyde by Govan shipbuilders and launched by the Queen Mother, in September 1986. In 1993, for cargo service only, the *Norbank* entered service. She is too big to enter the King George dock so operates from a new riverside terminal. (P&O North Sea Ferries).